Sum

of

Grant
Ron Chernow

Conversation Starters

By BookHabits

Please Note: This is an unofficial conversation starters guide. If you have not yet read the original work or would like to read it again, get the book here.

Copyright © 2017 by BookHabits. All Rights Reserved.

First Published in the United States of America 2017

We hope you enjoy this complementary guide from BookHabits.

Our mission is to aid readers and reading groups with quality, thought provoking material to in the discovery and discussions on some of today's favorite books.

Disclaimer / Terms of Use: Product names, logos, brands, and other trademarks featured or referred to within this publication are the property of their respective trademark holders and are not affiliated with BookHabits. The publisher and author make no representations or warranties with respect to the accuracy or completeness of these contents and disclaim all warranties such as warranties of fitness for a particular purpose. This guide is unofficial and unauthorized. It is not authorized, approved, licensed, or endorsed by the original book's author or publisher and any of their licensees or affiliates.

No part of this publication may be reproduced or retransmitted, electronic or mechanical, without the written permission of the publisher.

Tips for Using BookHabits Conversation Starters:

EVERY GOOD BOOK CONTAINS A WORLD FAR DEEPER THAN the surface of its pages. The characters and their world come alive through the words on the pages, yet the characters and its world still live on. Questions herein are designed to bring us beneath the surface of the page and invite us into the world that lives on. These questions can be used to:

- Foster a deeper understanding of the book
- Promote an atmosphere of discussion for groups
- Assist in the study of the book, either individually or corporately
- Explore unseen realms of the book as never seen before

About Us:

THROUGH YEARS OF EXPERIENCE AND FIELD EXPERTISE, from newspaper featured book clubs to local library chapters, *BookHabits* can bring your book discussion to life. Host your book party as we discuss some of today's most widely read books.

Table of Contents

Introducing *Grant* 6

Discussion Questions 16

Introducing the Author 37

Fireside Questions 42

Quiz Questions 53

Quiz Answers 66

Ways to Continue Your Reading 67

Introducing *Grant*

RON CHERNOW'S LATEST NOVEL, *GRANT*, IS about historical figure Ulysses S. Grant. It is a large book with around one thousand pages. Grant was the military general who won the Civil War. In *Grant*, Chernow breaks down the Civil War. He discusses why the war started and what happened after the war ended. Chernow also talks about how white southerners view Grant and the Reconstruction that followed the war as foolish rather than a good change for the nation.

The Civil War began in April of 1861 when the Confederates went to Fort Sumter in South Carolina to attack. About a week after this attack, Grant wrote to his father saying that the only two parties that exist now are the Patriots and the Traitors. Grant was concerned about the war, but never seemed to be overly concerned about the South's secession. Because Grant was the only man in Galena, Illinois that had a military background, he was nominated by the local militia's captain to recruit men for the war. Grant believed that most of the war would be fought by volunteer soldiers rather than trained soldiers who made a career out of being in the military.

    Grant's recruitment efforts were successful. He was able to recruit a company quickly, and he became the captain of this troops. He led these men into Springfield, Illinois. Governor Richard Yates offered to give Grant aid to train the volunteer soldiers, and Grant accepted this help. In June of 1861, Grant became a Colonel. His task as Colonel was to train the 21st Illinois Infantry, which was a troop of volunteer soldiers known for being rowdy. He was known for his heavy drinking, but this did not stop him from earning promotions in the military. Eventually, Grant was transferred to Missouri's Northern region in May of 1861 where he was given another promotion to Brigadier General.

During the Civil War, gaining control of the Mississippi River was important. At this point, Grant was seen as a leader with "iron will." He was given a command post in Cairo, Illinois at the

Mississippi River toward the end of August in 1861. Grant was moved into Paducah, Kentucky when the Confederates moved into Western Kentucky. It was important to President Lincoln to keep Kentucky as part of the Union. When Grant moved into Paducah, he told the residents there hat he came into their city as a friend, not an enemy.

In November of 1861, Grant was ordered to attack the Confederate soldiers in Belmont, Missouri. Grant and his troops were able to take the Confederate camp, but the Confederates forced them to retreat. He later was able to capture Fort Henry in 1862 with Andrew H. Foote, the Navy Flag Officer. This was an easy victory for Grant's troops, and they set their sights on capturing Fort Donelson.

However, the military at Fort Donelson was equal to Grant's troops. They had to retreat when they tried to attack and lost many of their soldiers in the battle. Soon after, more troops arrived. Grant and Foote, along with McClerndan and Wallace, attacked Fort Donelson again. This time they were able to take Fort Donelson. This was the first major win for Grant. President Lincoln promoted Grant to Major General.

At the Battle of Shiloh, Grant was ordered to wait for Major General Buell to arrive before he attacked. However, Grant's troops were subject to a surprise attack by the Confederate military. They were forced to retreat. Grant once believed this battle would end the war, but later realized his error and that the Union would have to take the Confederates completely in order to live. The next day, the troops of Buell and Wallace arrived. They attacked the Confederates and won, but it was the deadliest battle of the Civil War with nearly 24,000 casualties. In November of 1862, after President Lincoln read his Emancipation Proclamation, Grant issued an order that former slaves should be allowed to fight with the Union Army. He also gave these former slaves shelter, clothing, and wages in return for their military service.

After the Vicksburg Campaign and the Chattanooga Campaign, Grant was promoted by President Lincoln to Lieutenant General. This promotion occurred in March of 1864. This gave

Grant complete command of all of the Union Armies. At this point in time, Grant would only take orders from President Lincoln. Later that year, Grant fought Robert E. Lee and his troops in the Battle of Cold Harbor. He was able to capture some important railroad links during this battle. He used the railroad to continually attack Lee's troops. Though, he lost many men in this battle due to poor leadership using an explosion to blow up the Confederate trenches. Grant then defeated the Confederate Army at Nashville. This was a serious blow the Confederate troops. The only obstacle in their way of victory was Robert E. Lee.

In March of 1865, Lee's troops had been seriously weakened by the troops of Grant.

Thousands of members of Lee's troops deserted because they were hungry, and fighting a war in the trenches was difficult. The Union was able to take over Petersburg, Richmond, and Appomattox from the Confederates in April of 1865. Grant sent word to Lee asking him to surrender. Lee formally surrendered to Grant on April 9, 1985. Grant later expressed his feelings about Lee, saying that he had a large amount of dignity who fought valiantly for a long time. Grant granted Lee and his troops amnesty, but also asked the members of the Confederate troops to give up their weapons and go home. They were allowed to keep their horses as a long as hey promised they would never rebel against the government of the United States again.

Grant told his own troops that they should not celebrate the victory anymore and regard the Confederates as their fellow countrymen once again. Over the next several weeks, more Confederate forces came to surrender.

Five days after Grant took Appomattox from the Confederates, he was asked by President Lincoln to attend Ford's Theater. He and his wife declined the invitation, however, as they already had plans for the evening. This was the night that President Lincoln was assassinated inside the theater. Grant, and many other people believed that Grant was one of the targets in the plot devised by John Wilkes Booth. At Lincoln's funeral, Grant was visibly upset and called Lincoln one of the best men he ever knew.

He did not approve of President Andrew Johnson taking over and stated that the Reconstruction was set back under Johnson's administration.

In 1868, Ulysses S. Grant was elected the 18th President of the United States. He defeated his opponent Horatio Seymour with 214 electoral college votes to Seymour's 80 electoral college votes. The 15th Amendment, giving people of any race the right to vote, was ratified under President Grant. He continued to push for Reconstruction in the United States as President. President Grant was elected to a second term in 1872.

Discussion Questions

"Get Ready to Enter a New World"

Tip: Begin with questions dealing with broader issues to ensure ample time for quality discussions. Read through all discussion questions before engaging.

~~~

question 1

Consider your knowledge of Ulysses S. Grant before reading *Grant*. What did you learn about him from reading? How did your opinion change about him after reading?

~~~

question 2

It was well known that Ulysses S. Grant was a heavy drinker of alcohol. However, this did not stop him from being promoted nor did he get removed from his position or the military. Why do you think he was still able to earn promotions despite this fact?

~~~

question 3

Grant arrived in Paducah, Kentucky and told the residents there that he was their friend and not their enemy. Why do you think he did this?

~~~

~~~

question 4

It was important to President Lincoln to keep Kentucky as part of the Union. Why do you think this was so important?

~~~

~~~

question 5

In a letter to his father, Grant wrote that the only two sides now were Patriots and Traitors. Why do you think he felt this way?

~~~

question 6

Grant found himself leading the recruitment efforts in Illinois because he was the only person with a military background in the area. What do you think of this method of choosing a leader? How well do you think Grant did as a military leader even though he did not have a leadership background?

~~~

question 7

It appears that Grant was good friends with President Lincoln. What are your thoughts on their relationship?

~~~

question 8

Compare *Grant* to other biographies you have read. How does *Grant* rate among other biographies.

~~~

question 9

In one message to the Grand Army of the Republic, Grant said that though the men may never look at his face or hear his voice again, they still held a place in his heart, and he considered them his children. Why do you think he felt this way?

~~~

~~~

question 10

Grant was seen as a sad man. Considering what you have learned about Grant, what do you think made him sad?

~~~

~~~

question 11

Consider what you know about the time period portrayed in *Grant*. How accurately do you think Ron Chernow write about this time period?

~~~

question 12

Civil Rights, Reconstruction, and the 15th Amendment seem to be important issues to Grant. Why do you think these issues were so important to him?

~~~

question 13

Consider the career of Grant. Would you say he was successful because of his own efforts or the mistakes of the men he was fighting against?

~~~

~~~

question 14

When Andrew Johnson was sworn in as President after Lincoln's assassination, Grant said that Reconstruction was set back a long way. Why do you think he felt this way about Johnson's presidency?

~~~

~~~

question 15

Consider what you knew about the Civil War before reading *Grant*. What did you learn about the Civil War? How did your opinion change about the war after reading *Grant*?

~~~

~~~

question 16

Several readers have commented on the length of *Grant*. What are your thoughts on the books length?

~~~

~~~

question 17

Newsday called *Grant* an "essential read." How important do you think this book is?

~~~

~~~

question 18

Compelling and fascinating were two words that *BookPage* used to describe *Grant*. What was your reading experience like?

~~~

~~~

question 19

One critique of *Grant* was that Ron Chernow does not admit to Grant's flaws in his book. While other readers feel as though Chernow accurately represented Grant, flaws and all. What are your thoughts on this topic?

~~~

~~~

question 20

One reader recommended this book to readers who enjoy reading about historical figures and events. Who would you recommend this book to?

~~~

Introducing the Author

RON CHERNOW WAS BORN ON MARCH 3, 1949 in New York City, New York. He is best known for being an author, biographer, historian, and journalist. Several of his books have won awards. In 2011, he was the recipient of the Pulitzer Prize for Biography for his book *Washington: A Life*.

Ron Chernow was he son of Israel and Ruth Chernow. Israel owned a discount store. He also founded a firm that did stock brokerage. Ruth earned a living as a bookkeeper. His family is Jewish. Politically, he considers himself to be a Democrat, and he describes himself as "disgruntled."

Chernow attended Yale College where he graduated *summa cum laude* and earned a Bachelor of Arts Degree in 1970. He also attended Pembroke College, which is part of Cambridge University. At Pembroke, he earned a Master's of Philosophy Degree in 1972. He attempted to earn a Doctorate Degree for himself. However, he was not able to complete the coursework for this degree. Chernow has also earned honorary degrees from Skidmore College, Marymount Manhattan College, Hamilton College, Long Island University, and Washington College. He married his wife, Valerie, in 1979. She worked at the New York City College of Technology where she taught Social Sciences and Languages as an assistant professor. Sadly, his wife passed away in January of 2006.

In his career life, Chernow started working as a freelance journalist. He wrote for several different magazines from 1973 until 1982. In 1986, he began to focus more on his own writing. Chernow's first book, *The House of Morgan*, was published in 1990. This nonfiction book follows the J.P. Morgan financial group for four generations. It was awarded the National Book Award for Nonfiction.

Chernow's second book, *The Warburgs*, is about the Warburg family, who were Jewish. They left Germany and came to the United States in 1938. *The Warburgs* was published in 1993. It was considered by the American Library Association as one of the top ten books that year. It was also considered a Notable Book by *The New York Times*. In 1997, Chernow released a collection of essays entitled *The Death of the Banker*. The following year he published the biography, *Titan: The Life of John D. Rockefeller, Sr.* This biography was considered to be one of the years top ten books by *The New York Times* and *Time*. It was a bestseller for *The New York Times* for sixteen weeks.

In 2004, Chernow began writing political biographies. His first release in this category was *Alexander Hamilton*. This biography was a bestseller for *The New York Times* for three months. It also won the George Washington Book Prize and was nominated for the National Book Critics Award in 2004. *Alexander Hamilton* was adapted into a musical by Lin-Manuel Miranda. *Hamilton*, the musical, opened in 2015 on Broadway and won a Tony award.

Washington: A Life, Chernow's sixth book release was published in 2010. It was awarded the American History Book Prize and the Pulitzer Prize. Chernow's latest book release was *Grant*, about the life of Ulysses S. Grant. Chernow signed a deal to write the book in 2011, and it was finally published in 2017.

Fireside Questions

"What would you do?"

Tip: These questions can be a fun exercise as it spurs creativity among the readers by allowing alternate scene endings and "if this was you" questions.

~~~

question 21

Ron Chernow has made a name for himself as a biographer. How well do you think he writes a biography?

~~~

~~~

question 22

It took Chernow six years to write *Grant* after the deal was signed for him to write it. Why do you think it took so long?

~~~

~~~

question 23

Chernow started a doctorate degree but did not finish it. Why do you think this is?

~~~

~~~

question 24

Several of Chernow's books have been given prestigious awards. Why do you think this is?

~~~

~~~

question 25

Chernow is known for writing nonfiction and historical biographies. Why do you think he has chosen to stay in this genre?

~~~

~~~

question 26

Imagine the Civil War took place in the 2010s. How would it be different than in the 1860s?

~~~

~~~

question 27

Imagine you were a leader during the Civil War. What would be your strategy to victory?

~~~

question 28

Consider the possibility that the Confederate side won the Civil War. What would the United States look like if they had won?

question 29

Imagine you are the author of *Grant*. How would you write this book differently than Chernow did?

question 30

Grant is a biography that totals nearly one thousand pages. How would this book be different if it had half the number of pages?

Quiz Questions

"Ready to Announce the Winners?"

Tip: Create a leaderboard and track scores to see who gets the most correct answers. Winners required. Prizes optional.

~~~

quiz question 1

The subject of Ron Chernow's latest novel is Ulysses S. Grant. Grant was a military general who won the _____ War.

~~~

~~~

quiz question 2

The Civil War began in April of _____. At this point in time, the Confederates attacked Fort Sumter.

~~~

quiz question 3

Grant and his men faced a surprise attack by the Confederate soldiers at the Battle of _____. However, he was able to defeat the Confederates the next day with the help of Buell and Wallace.

quiz question 4

Grant was promoted to _____ after the Vicksburg Campaign and the Chattanooga Campaign. He would only take orders from President Lincoln after this.

~~~

quiz question 5

True or False: Robert E. Lee was able to defeat Grant. This led to the Confederates winning the Civil War.

~~~

~~~

quiz question 6

True or False: Grant was asked by President Lincoln to be his guest at the Ford's Theater the night Lincoln was assassinated. Grant, and many others, believed that he was a target that night.

~~~

quiz question 7

True or False: Grant ran for President in 1868. However, he was defeated by Horatio Seymour.

~~~

quiz question 8

Ron Chernow was born in _____. He is best known for being an author, biographer, historian, and journalist.

~~~

~~~

quiz question 9

At _____ College, Chernow earned his Bachelor of Arts Degree. He graduated *summa cum laude*.

~~~

~~~

quiz question 10

Before becoming an author, Chernow worked as a freelance _____. He wrote for many magazines from 1973 to 1982.

~~~

~~~

quiz question 11

True or False: Chernow's first book was *The House of Morgan*. It was given the National Book Award for Nonfiction.

~~~

~~~

quiz question 12

True or False: Chernow published his sixth book, *Washington: A Life*, in 2010. This book won him the Pulitzer Prize for Biography.

~~~

Quiz Answers

1. Civil
2. 1861
3. Shiloh
4. Lieutenant General
5. False; Grant weakened Lee's troops. Then, Grant asked Lee to surrender.
6. True
7. False; Grant ran for President in 1868. He defeated Seymour by a landslide and became President.
8. New York
9. Yale
10. Journalist
11. True
12. True

Ways to Continue Your Reading

EVERY month, our team runs through a wide selection of books to pick the best titles for readers and reading groups, and promotes these titles to our thousands of readers – sometimes with free downloads, sale dates, and additional brochures.

If you have not yet read the original work or would like to read it again, get the book here.

Want to register yourself or a book group? It's free and takes 1-click.

Register here.

On the Next Page…

Please write us your reviews! Any length would be fine but we'd appreciate hearing you more! We'd be SO grateful.

Till next time,

BookHabits

"Loving Books is Actually a Habit"

Lightning Source UK Ltd.
Milton Keynes UK
UKHW010653300519
343596UK00001B/406/P